KOHL AND CHALK

KOHL AND CHALK

POEMS

by

Shadab Zeest Hashmi

POETIC MATRIX PRESS

ISBN: 978-0-9852883-9-6

Poetic Matrix Press
www.poeticmatrix.com

ACKNOWLEDGEMENTS

Deepest thanks to all my mentors, in particular Lisa Steinman, Eleanor Wilner, Sandra Alcosser, Ansa Zafar, Sam Hamill, Maurice Manning and Heather McHugh, and poet-friends Karen Kenyon, Ishmael Von Heidrick-Barnes, Mandy Brauer, Ilona Yusuf and Brandon Cesmat who have known and nurtured these poems for many years, in many places—from Lahore to Portland, San Diego to Ashville. A salute to Shameem, my husband, who shares all my places - on the map or off!

Thanks, also, to the editors of the journals where these poems were first published:

The Adirondack Review
Vallum
RHINO
The Bitter Oleander
Nimrod International
Hubbub
Pakistaniaat: A Journal of Pakistan Studies
The Citron Review
Solidarity International
New Millennium Writings
Pakistani Literature
UniVerse: A United Nations of Poets
Journal of Postcolonial Writings
San Diego Poetry Annual
Poetic Medicine
Journal of Contemporary World Literature
Poetry Conspiracy

Kohl, to see the moon lucid, to let place
dream you up — Chalk, to map that dream,
to draw cross hatched lanterns
and mirrors between borders.

For Salma and Muhammad
My parents
Who taught me to see,
to map.

Contents

KOHL AND CHALK

Window in Chalk

Her Ancient Samovar

KOHL AND CHALK

I LOOK OUT THE MUGHAL WINDOW

In the last dream the *sanwayan* was hot but no one was hungry. I heard
a cackle while I waited for my husband to finish the teakwood shelf, the
day already topaz and breaking. Who was it? The washerwoman or a
mountain magpie? I looked out the window of the Mughal tower,
carved with flowers. For a moment I thought I saw a wisp of yellow hair
on the polished tiles down below. Perhaps it was brushed aside by the
breeze. Some of the cobalt and turquoise tiles had split. There was much
that needed mending. Our sons would fix walls damaged by cherry
bombs and doors that were like sieves; so many bullets had passed
through them. Our daughters would inscribe from memory all that our
burnt books had contained. Long after the attack, the latticed pillars
remained scented with *chambeli* buds. We had just begun whitewashing
the house for the wedding, when they came again. Later, the bride sifted
through the rubble for *Rubaiyat,* the groom washed the *kulha* he had
meant to wear for the ceremony, its gold woven cloth grimy for once in
hundreds of years. The shadows are bayonets, rhino horns. We are
never safe when feasts are offered us on the heads of *naags.* We see
shadows darting. What they steal most is our work, so we never have
time to sit together and eat. We strain to write down each syllable our
elders left us. Our children do not laugh any more. Our supper gets cold,
uneaten.

CARDAMOM EYES

FACIAL PALSY

*B*ut now, the tailor in the verandah and a pool of trousseau silk and
chiffon like the gauzy mist of Chinese calendars, the sewing machine
racing along a *Noor jehani kameez,* I face you, you, half frozen like a
fairytale-curse, one eye a cold star, lips part-numb, split into your lit and
dim halves by the gold and ruby *tika,* the bride's jewel that sits on the
forehead, hanging delicate from a string of pearls. I'm claiming you. In
this blue-tiled bathroom, window sunlit, the swaying plum tree caught
in my mirror like a feather-fan this November morning, I'm claiming
you as mine. In the last two days, I've become used to letting my thoughts
run to the sound of the sewing machine. In the last two days you've left
me more alone than I felt when one morning I was forgotten in an
orange tub in the lawn until night had fallen, until a star had appeared
on the wall between the kitchen garden and the lawn in the shape of the
woolen lion-man of my brother's sweater: the knitted creature with a
fixed gaze, wild mane. Only a dream; a time I had my own sewing
machine with a red polka-dot top that said "petit" in plump letters; only a
toy. And you, face, feeble as falling ash, an eggshell when it breaks for
trembling new chicks, a treble that even the swift air won't carry, one
half of you abandoned, its muscles the weight of lead, dragging to keep
up with the sprightly half. There is rouge from Paris, coconut oil from
Orissa, Turkish bracelets, flame-colored roses from the garden, the
sewing machine's crescendo. Soon the bridal dress will arrive, and
jewelry and high heels and henna. I'm cupping your grief and filling
with it the hollows, the penny art of my soul. I'm claiming you now like
never before.

WEDDING GHAZAL

They said, "a fistful of rice!" Instead, I threw a glance
over my shoulder at the thin copper mist, at my city diluting.

Everything was in need of a bride's blessing: forts, schools,
buses, stationery shops, even the Indus in the distance, diluting.

My dowry was a silk cap with geometrically broken hearts,
sewn by Afghan refugees; in art's labor, their grief diluting.

A cap lined with Rumi's verses must find the poet-bride.
But all it found was a yellowed dream, its memory diluting.

Look, the calm of the yogurt sellers, magazine vendors
before the bomb-blast, and afterwards, all peace diluting.

Do not forget, Zeest, the green-guava scent of this town
or the beauty of labor, as your groom sees your henna diluting.

Poem for a Wedding Feast

Wet henna on one hand
The other wedded to a seashell pen
fingers hooked
into its shimmering ochre vertebrae

Midnight
come leak through the ball-point
before coriander melts with ginger
and the aluminum pot growls like a hunting dog

Come when cuts are sealed
knives washed
burns doused in almond oil
Come when Clorox fades
and jasmine rises

Bring the grumbling muse
Meet me by the needlepoint ivy
plaited with blunt phrases
slack moon beams

Taste-buds Bloom on Silence

A poem for three voices

Great links from column to column

Beautiful

Dark honey		
For the newly born		
Silvery cakes for the bride		
For the groom		
Rose pistachio milk		
Rice pudding		
for when we gather	Rice pudding for when	
	we gather	Sweet rice pudding
		Almonds and cream
		Sweet rice pudding
		Golden green pistachios
	Sweet rice pudding	
	for when we gather	
Roses for the newly-wed		
Roses for the long dead		
Roses for when we get		Orange-red roses
together		For when we gather
		Velvet-dark roses
		For when we gather
	Marble-red roses	
	And moon-soft jasmines	Yellow shiny rice
		Dark sugar
		Almonds sprinkled
		Star formations
	Star formations	
	Constellations	
Fate		
This night sky	Fate	
	This dark sugar sky	Fate
		This night sky
	Fate	
	This night sky	
For when we gather		
Roses		
For when we gather		
Rice		We gather
	We gather	
Under the night sky		
A trail of petals	Under the night sky	The scent
		Of warm rice
	Under the sugar sky	

Pungent and cold	We gather	Night sky
Pungent and cold Sweets Worth their weight in silver And gold	Pungent and cold	Pungent and cold?
Falling On the tongue Like a curse	Curse	

Falling heavy
   Falling like metal
In the mouth
   Cutting its way
	Heavy
	Heavy
	Heavy
	Into the abyss
	The empty heart
		Where is the heart?

Night sky smudged Marble-red	Where is the heart?	
Sweetness torn	The heart	Where is the heart?
Silver dark thorn	The heart	Night-dew This night sky
	Slippery dark petals	
Red petals Elongate like ear lobes Disappear		How do they disappear?

Like silence into many
  silences
	They disappear	Like silence
		   the metal mouth burns
		Ear lobes
		   Elongate
		Touch the ground

Bury sound Deep in the ground	Deep dirt ground	Under this sugar sky
Silence probing the heart	The heart Earth heart	
Honey dark heart Birthing bent heart	Silence borne of earth	Earth heart Heart grows silent

[handwritten margin notes: "loses cadence + Focus"; "Heavy Hurled"]

11

Dark honey heart
    Silence - burnt heart
Silence turned heart
 	
Sweets for the child
Sweets for the bride
And for the groom
And for when we meet
 	
Sweet silent heart
    Honey dark heart
Rose gloom heart
	
	Bloom heart *too*
	Bloom heart
	Bloom *Much?*
		Out of silence
		Sweets
		
		Earth born sweet
		
		Bloom

HOW TO CARE FOR A POET

Discard old sponges. Wash her bitter with dried gourd.
This, to surface the memory of aniseed—
She has walked down a staircase all night. Each step was a NO.
Be a tall window in her dream. A light
that rises from basement to terrace.
Pick thorns from her hair,
spasms from her ankle. She abides
in a storm, her suitcase full of stopped
clocks. Paste a Persian garden
on her door, a gazebo of swans.
Promise her wild grass
and oil lamps. Fold her at least nine times
in the crushed velvet you found her in. Keep
her aglow with moth wings.

Creative, but a bit mannered in its freshness. Great
control of tone.

APRIL

Wild flowers are looming
over gutters
Monarchs and viceroys flicker
past cracked pavements
Someone planted silence
where a word should have been
How it grows
A farmer calls his old truck
brown sugar
I recall a three-legged dog with another sweet name
The soul mercuries and lifts itself
to the sleepy berry-blue

This has been a long day
You would think it ends
with the soul all poured into your strong patient hands
pure yellow like the very sun's powder

[handwritten note: — Shift from declarative statements to conditional ✓]

14

TACITURNUS

*A*ll that silence has uttered so far
is creased in the mystique of your hand
where we understand
like a burst of lightning
faint and deep
fate-lines run into each other
gasping at every collision

It is not the clouds that pass shadows
on your face but the stillness of light
A sunny sky if empty of moving light
wrenches as much cheer
as the overcast day
or your fretting

And so it is neither the sun nor the road
shooting fast like a lizard's tongue
that changes the shape or color or depth
of the shadows
on your face
A prelude to silence
As still as the tidy labyrinth of spiral lines
on the tips of your fingers

I WISHED TO WRITE YOU AN AUBADE

Instead of walking the night in Paris,
letting our eyes be the sharply defined pansies
the nasal city has so longed for,
we shut ourselves in a room
that was no friend,
and carved one argument after another.
Instead of gazing
at the Mona Lisa in the Louvre,
we bought a black and white print
(of a man climbing a coconut palm)
from a youth who claimed
that the money will go to a scholarship fund.
We hoped never to be friendless or in need.

What was there about the place
but loftiness? A mistaken sense of perfume.
Less distinct than lulling. So we went
to the marketplace which smelled of cheese.
Flat, cold fish. And swollen bread.

I wished to write you an aubade.
Instead, I gazed at the early morning river
lit by Impressionistic dots of light
through the life-size glass
of the train door,
and your reflection superimposed on it.

LABOR AND DELIVERY

The night is a cold sack
in room 302 where red and green lights are blinking
like wild berries tossed from their tree in lightning
Graphs emerge on scrolls
sharp as alligator teeth
on paper unrolling forever.
Listen I am a paper kite in your hands
and this room is a star-gazer's hill
Beyond these Dopplers and monitors
are the creamy shadows of passing moons
feathery comets with soft light funneling through
Call me with the slightest tug
in your own sweet time   — To The child

GHAZAL FOR THE NINTH MONTH

Your august birth, my taking oath as an American, were only weeks apart.
The most I can remember is your rocking to a dull ache before we were apart.

Our hill was plush, the whole place soaked up the scent of raisin *pulao.* On
the last day of July the umbilical cord was cut, yet still we were barely apart.

I had sworn to bear arms for this country. A cat prowled between the young
apple tree and dry lobelia; camouflaged, I couldn't tell her parts apart.

I acted mother first when I frantically covered you, half-dreaming you were
the tender bird of prey and a feline form was the country of which I was a part.

Bear arms? Kill like a predator? In other dreams I bore you through the cold months,
through snow in Julian, rain in Sedona. Not for a single minute were we apart.

This ties together

NAMING THE BABY

Who knows what you hear;
Music made by djinns in an old vinegar bottle,
seismic messages between elephants,
a butterfly opening its fine-spun wings
like a book hot off the press?
Your eyes are a winter lake, their hazel secretive, now smoky,
now clear, as you watch a lone duck fly.
You know me by scent and you mistake no one
for me, *liebe*, like *haleeb*, like lips latched.
I'd name you for the bird you watch so intently,
but you are more
Mikyle, angel of rain
and daily bread.

(liebe: German for love
haleeb: Arabic for milk)

NOTES FOR MY HUSBAND

I showed Yousuf to the amethyst
Morning when he was born

Kettledrums play four at a time
Each tuned to play its own note
Each he would swallow whole
With my vertical voice in Urdu

And watch with his cardamom eyes
The slow flare of Van Gogh's Sun Flowers
The silk ascent to Victoria's Peak
The concave shine of mango *achar*

He is slender like pine nuts
And keen on butter

Yaseen prefers honey
And tells me the sun on the front door
Smells like library soap
I feel the light lathering the knob
As I open it

The house is filled
With jazz and bag-pipes
Iqbal's poems
On marble construction paper

We weep in both languages
And anything round is a planet

THUNDERCLAP

The dunes moved with the night's wind
the oasis and the blooms

The small pattern on the drawer liner
wick of the four-hour blueberry candle
baby's chapped skin
the brown shoe lace with one plastic tail missing
the thunderclap with two of my beats in its heart
which never awakened you
      (the pine book shelf under the bed
          the taco shells that stayed in the pantry
             four years after the expiration date)
               All this was life

And where was love?

Gulped in by the wash basin every night
you brushed your teeth and every morning
when words are a dream-filled mist in your mouth
Where was love?
In the air surrounding the house
scented with laundry detergent
The ribbon of steam that came spectacular as a comet
when the dryer was on
In a crease of the starry sky
waiting to magnify
in pools of rain water
at your feet

You always kept them dry

THIRTEENTH ANNIVERSARY

The years click like prayer beads
in the quiet hours of a marble mosque
like coins from every corner
of the world falling back into gold mines

Everything wished for us
by our mothers
remains sewn into our hems
despite hurricanes tearing our clothes
or the dirty iguana that sleeps
along the entire length
of the clothesline

SUCH AS THE WEIGHT OF SALT
ON A FLAME

such as the long surviving flower
in a bottle of cream
soda, the strategy
of termites, song of melting ice,
a brush
living for seventeen years in nail paint,
such as the voice we use for taxi drivers,
such as please,
I must migrate
It is spring and I can hear in the wind
the wings   NO!
of my fellow-butterflies.

MIRRORWORK, SLINGSHOT

LAB

Earth and water and fire must burn
here forever in the hope of a birth

This is the room I walked in
thinking how cold despite all the burning

Thinking it's a gray eye
all vacancy and chill and silence without contours

Poetry was shattering itself outside the window
waiting for a word

And I left
the flasks and test tubes to be broken
by the silence

BILINGUAL

In the butcher's window
there were tongues
marinating in oils
& auspicious herbs
I said
that one with the rainbow

& if I may have two
give me that other
that many-textured one
crisp & tight & sublime
supple like tapioca
fine-edged like a prince's dagger

& reversible
like a damask sash

& grooved like the pit
of a peach
please

He filled my greedy mouth
with two
half-tongues

IT'S YOUR MARMALADE HOUSE

where the goats are the sentries

Tonight's turnip stew
is burning
while you read a *masnavi*
lying on a rope cot

I'm on a rickety stool
threatening to break
prayer beads

I break your fountain pen
wipe off the ink on your curtains
and with the celerity of a djinn
climb the roof

causing dusty pigeons to flutter

From here I see kites teasing
fallen feathers
I see our sentries
dozing

Look how my suddenness
has tripped time itself

for the house
was sold
twenty years ago when you died

MONSOON

(handwritten: ✓ complicated)

Why the pale mosquito net
over the *charpai* I slept on all summer
still falls liquid in my memory
like sugar cane juice
or why the *Polonaise*
is like running along the small green humps
of a single hill in Europe
where no one dies of summer *(handwritten: —? unlike there)*
I don't know
But when the sky growls
and lightning crackles its long plastic fingers
the dusty *jamun* is less ghost
more tree *(handwritten: ✓)*
the city baked hollow in the sun's furnace
sprouts double-shaded roses
When the rains come
I bring Socrates
from the glass shelves
cut a mango in cubes to go with some milk
There is no need for Chopin
because the young Afghan from the refugee camp
(who made himself
a wheel chair after the war) *(handwritten: Is a surprising grim image)*
plays his flute all day long
to the rain's vigorous beat

Finger Painting

Night slips down the windshield,
despite street lamps and the crooked moon
behind a blue yolk of clouds.
Covered, I can now recall
what usually brings with it fear;
the story of Cleopatra's death
or how an old man broke a promise
and how a child's ghost never forgave him.
A soft rain shadow
rolling silently on the thick glass
suddenly shrieks and splits
where a stray bullet had once made
a see-through crater.
        I remember how a crippled child
peeled a tangerine one December morning,
and how the citrus dew made a strange mist
in the sun, and how it took only a moment
for this sweet, wet dust to disappear
the way the shiny toy had disappeared
when he had reached for it,
back when he was in Kabul.
That is how the Russians had burnt
a little boy's limbs.
        I remember his eyes: Indus-blue and lost.
Rain shadows crawl softly over the night
like huge peacock feathers.
And softly,
the rain layers itself under the skin of memory,
as paper drinks paint off of my fingers.

31

Radio Moscow

Peshawar, 1987

With a poem in my pocket
I stand under the rain-drummed roof

I am still
trying to remember

Let's call suffering
by the stone's name
and the moon petrifying
in my other pocket

will perhaps stir
I wake to Radio Moscow
and the train does not stop

I am
still trying to remember

ghosts
the space between news and songs
voices in mud

I am
still tying

bells around
Angora goats

between bombings
trying to remember — *Trying too hard?*

COLORING THE BORDER

They stood in cleanest sunlight,
the mountains,
their lines so cold
there wasn't a color for them in my pencil box.

I let the sharp breeze cut out
emerald for a heart
with a *pushto* beat,
a tribe lost and hanging by the star of David,
a language blue and gold-veined like lapis,
I drew war cries of the Greeks
in plume-red,
the Mongols in horse-leather red.

It was 1979,
history looping
like a bomb circuit,
feeding on itself,
while the black curve of *Tor Khum*,
a trail of loss,
sang in war-tongues,
a lament drained of all color.

When I left,
I left for long and with
my pencil box.

(*Tor Khum* or *The Black Curve* is a small town on the northwestern border between Pakistan and Afghanistan.)

Stepping Across the Border

From my home window
   Prussian blue
Mazda's window
   broken glass blue
my school's window
   carbon-paper blue

Mountains
   circled my life like a spell
in blue

At *Tor Khum*
   they were touching distance
Was it charcoal or chalk or rope
   that marked the border?
Afghanistan was just beyond a slim crease of blue

Before being warned by the guards
   I had moved my foot across
To step into what would later become ash blue

The guards made me step back
   gave me a watermelon
I was only a child under the spell of mountains
   Out of which I would later see
refugees flow
   River blue   Bruise blue

Writing to My Maker
from the Café
Between Afghanistan and Pakistan

King of clocks, king
of moving clouds,
and of everything still,
roaming, flint-mouthed, raw,
quiet,
everything dribbling over the green
threshold
of birth, everything in the soft
cavity
of waste

There is nothing I want more
than to give you
for safekeeping
this view of rocky mountains,
our table by the window,
a flimsy egg-sandwich
and a bottle of Coca Cola

Nothing more than the comfort
that the menu here
will always be given in the fresh
scribble of a voice
with no more than two items

And on the drive home
to Peshawar,
there will always be the muscular lift
of the Khyber Pass
And the sleep
that comes
only to happy children.

PASSING THROUGH PESHAWAR

I know each poplar and willow of this town,
how telephone wires sag with the weight of belligerent crows,
the Tonga-horses wait at red lights.
I know afternoon shadows on slate verandahs,
the squeaking of a rusted seesaw,

the breaking open of a walnut in a door-hinge;
its embossed shell, a secret cracking;

the winter sun warming the mosque's marble,
plums sold in crates on the roadside,
corn with salt and lime,
the radio at the *tandoor* playing
filmi songs, the whiff of Lux soap.

I almost say to you,
Look out the window,
look, look, look!
My library with beetle-eaten furniture,
my raw silk bazaar, my ancient fort!
And look, the bakery that sells pink coconut rolls!
And look, there I used to get my hair cut.

One turn and my town will once again
socket into its timeless hollow
what I remember, what I know.
The bus will pass
all these things
before you click pause on your video game. — Discontent

36

WINDOW IN CHALK

DEBUT

In the clutches of dried-up ivy, a shut window
reflects an "open" sign
with a real powder-blue sky as backdrop.

Fastened by ivy's twisted ropes,
showing light as if from the world
framed in sea-green shutters,
this window is quenching my *sufi* thirst,
offering a clear cup of sky to drink from.

If there is a soul,
it has stepped out of its tight shoes
for the first time
and, whirling to the sky's delight, finds itself
at 4:50 pm, in this noise-filled pocket of Paris.

In Bangkok

We say no to the boy selling paper parasols.
In the tropics, paper sweats and wilts, temples
stand punished in the air stilted along the river.
Waiting for the boat, our children begin to whine.
I scold them in Urdu, give them a fish cracker each,
my husband reads aloud from the tour book the part
about the snake farm. Frantic for juice,
the children attract the attention of the man
ahead of us in line, who then produces
a piece of paper and starts drawing
with precision strokes: A lean fighter-plane
with a sickle lip, followed by another.
We smile in a foreign tongue. He says
he's from Israel. We say thank you
for the planes. When the man begins
to draw again, I say, how about a house
or a cat? He draws a house with no windows,
no doors, only a high wall, slanted roof.
I'm about to ask for windows when the boat arrives.
A sweet Hebrew school-boy, he had once chanted
in English class:
"Shut the door, shut the window" while outside,
F16s growled. He walks the earth now with a pencil,
doing away with doors and windows.

THE WINDOW IN THE CHINESE CHARACTER FOR HAPPINESS

Contains
acres of maize fields.
Black arms extended,
a woman in flight.
In weightless,
turmeric light,
a full rice-pot on the window sill.
You and I.

Pierre Bonnard's Open Window

Is vibrant. I shall whitewash
his room. And complete
the half-painting on the floor.
When I fall into the company of ghosts
on the terrace-library again,
I'll invite them through the window
of his studio.
And teach them to rewrite books.

(Taj Mahal)
The hundred-moon window

Would-be eye to my soul,
vacuous lot, stony chamber.
Eye to the innocence
of flowering marble.
The slow moon-beams
threading into Jamuna.
I, the betrayed,
beg for a window.

For *Taus,* my emeralded,
has thrown up gems
on to the plunderer's lap.
Sons, all enemies. Agra, fire
and deceit.

I, the emperor,
beg for a window.

HUNTING BY THE RAVI

Though the glow
is such a perfect amber
this instant and Ravi
swirling with Sanskrit
Turkish Arabic Punjabi
is the old river with many silk mouths
    Though *Kamran's bara-dari*
    each of its twelve doors open
     is ready as the sun sets
     as if the prince will step in
    any moment after the day's hunt
    his leather-lined boats still wafting
      around the island

There is terrible secrecy
Time hangs like the yellow air
Tentative as the half-lifted feet
of gazelle
    There is a silence so full of thirst
    you forget you are at the mouth
      of a river

Tar and smoke and dust
from trucks rickshaws pick-up vans
Persian Urdu English
Avenues stretch to Ravi
like burnt filaments
McLeod Road
Myan Meer
Anarkali bazaar
    Because this sixteenth century chamber
     is defined by doors
Because these doors have been open
for hundreds of years
    the winds blowing through them
     unshackling
We come here
to end the hunt

HER ANCIENT SAMOVAR

Ghazal

*W*as this not the garden of the crisp acorn and the dusty, bearded Oak?
We left paradise because justice was promised on the other side.

There was much wood to collect, so we cut down the oak, the teak,
the olive. The new bridge was burned before we reached the other side.

Who hung the garlands, snatched the rose from the lark's side?
With the sun arrived the moon-filled aubade, night's other side.

Strange how they thought to compensate me with two minutes of silence,
or replace you with pension, I on this side of the war and them, the other side.

Remember the broken sky, the terrible storm, animals tumbling
in the ark? It was a man of faith who carried them to the other side.

If ever there was a wish, it was this: Zeest, may you belong
to the one who knows to cherish you, this side of life and the other side.

PANTOUM IN BLUE

The silken threads of aqua, royal, sky
passed through their fingers like lakes. She left
them a needle with a hundred eyes;
a chill more piercing than Ladakh for the bereft.

Or the unaware passing through her valley like lakes, cleft
and alone. From her ancient samovar, they drank Darjeeling
to cure the chill more piercing than Ladakh for the bereft.
Weaving *Shatoosh*, their minds were locked, hers reeling.

From her ancient samovar, they drank Darjeeling,
As if it was mulberry for a silk worm's work.
Weaving *shatoosh*, their minds were locked, hers reeling.
She sewed ripe bruises, freed the purple work.

Watched by the needle with a hundred eyes,
they bared silken veins of aqua, royal and sky.

Knotted Ghazal

A prince's halted speech on Sinai; the palatine knot
undone with no wine: a divine double-knot.

The coral feet of pigeons, the shrine, the rot
of souls: low and lofty desires twined into a knot.

Prayers ricochet like mercury and moonshine; caught
together they crook, they columbine in a knot.

Fluted, domed temples (or candle-lit, crystalline) blot
out the destitute: Their fortunes defined by a knot.

Heaven, always straight up, is open to the disinclined lot
too, but Zeest, some can climb like a vine, knot by knot.

Old Delhi

The book has the proportions of a human
grave. People come in rickshaws
or on foot, lay marigolds, burn
incense. One page is a sigh,
the next a snarl. The centerfold
holds the poet's wish: May you read me long
and often. Near and far-
sighted alike bring their glasses,
leave a trail of clay lanterns –
from the cinemas and snack bars
to the alley
where a poet once
desired.

GUNGA DIN'S REVENGE

pull, predetermined

Gunga Din's ghost lifted from the tennis courts
of Peshawar Club, wrapped in a steel wind,
coiling itself neatly around
the BLACKS AND DOGS NOT ALLOWED sign.
By then the tommies whose throats he moistened,
whose boots he shined when he was alive, had had enough
of his black face appearing in their stew,
his low *Yes sir* from the next world
seeming to melt the colonel's crimson portrait
beside the dust-heavy curtains in the ball room.
In the nightly clatter of dinner on the lawns,
his seemed to be the sorry bone that cracked between
the stray cat's lightning-blue jaw. The tommies dropped
their cigars on the dew and forgot the word for water
in Urdu, faces pale as *naag champa* in moonlight,
syllables slipping like soap, like frogs on slick rocks, vowels
gaping at every bearer who brought them water.
When they had "wopped'im"
in the battlefield because he couldn't serve them all
Din mumbled *Sahib, please.* Din
took a bullet for the queen, but the dead men's boat
came back to the chipped paradise of her majesty,
bearing his ghost. "Injia's sunny" now
that Din's sent the tommies packing their tail coats,
their pistols, cigar boxes, and their idioms stained
with the blood of blacks and dogs.

51

SWAT

*C*ross hatched lantern:
Riddle of lodges, springs, *paan-cigarette* cabins,
tire shops,
chinar trees circled by the musk of kerosene
A ladder to the moon throws
the valley a spine-kissing shadow

I would have bottled the tingle in birdsong
eaten the coconut-white river
climbed the far end of the ladder

But parrots are squawking
I am summoned
to shoulder
this place like a pallbearer

THE ROAD

A muezzin rides his motorbike
to the mosque that will
by afternoon
melt
down to the last ablution
faucet or blade
of the ceiling fan
the last worshipper

Locked in by traffic:

an ambulance no one clears
the way for

The gaunt policeman's whistle
is for the errant rickshaw-driver
or students likely from the Arts or Pakistan Studies
departments
in their dilapidated models

At such intersections
there usually are boys
selling strings of jasmines for the wrist
or jute hand-fans
or the newspaper
that serves better as a hand-fan

It's over fifty degrees Celsius
which means death
for the sherbet vendor
who can no longer afford to buy
or keep ice
and the laborer
working the day shift

The MNA won't see this
through her Ferragamo sunglasses
and tinted windows
as she is rushed
from the Assembly House
for her salon appointment

The sirens of her police escort
will neatly bury
the cacophony
of the explosion
in the mosque

but she might notice a motorbike
with a *shopper* filled with mangoes
hanging on one side
and another with new sandals
for a boy
the same age as her own

(*muezzin*: One who calls the faithful to prayer
MNA: Member of the National Assembly
Shopper: Pakistani slang for a plastic shopping bag)

JINNAH'S TYPEWRITER

Your typewriter has been found
in a tangle of seaweed

clacking over the waves of the Arabian Sea
in sand-grit staccato

for sixty odd years
churning the same speech

first in the key
of partition trains rattling
with the dead
then the massacre of '71
the "hunter-killer"
MQ-nines

The sea
smooth as carbon paper
clones a speech with every wave:
Unity, Faith, Discipline

What was spilled
came back as hardened coral:

Each time a still-birth

Your typewriter keeps time
with the beggar-women
weeping
by the shore

(Jinnah, the founder of Pakistan, is said to have remarked that he made
Pakistan with the help of his sister and his typewriter.)

Fatima Jinnah Enters her Brother's Study

In your study
a large shadow spun of thought

What the camera will catch:
a lizard between window slats
curtains sighing
their dusty sighs
on fine porcelain
mother of pearl inlay
and ivory-handled things
Then rain slanting in
on leather trimmed
gilt-edged things

The camera will feed on nonsense
while the shadow stretches
long waking hours filled with work
hanging in corners

between the lips of monsoon-sagged
maps
half rolled

holding
but a wish

MALABAR HILLS

The old calendar hangs
   (Discolored sinewy horses
galloping above April/May)

Here
   a Raj-style chair
bovine calm of the moon
   and a glass leaning
emblazoned on the verandah

There is a kneecap in the word *diction*
   where memory collects
We walk on the unsayable

Such as:
   Honey tipped knife
Cancer cell pluralizing
   Marketplace/massacre/mosque
   Foliage/failure
Parched and hanging
Never tear the calendar

Let it always be early
spring. Bring your sugared
tea to the foot of the staircase

Jinnah's beloved home (Malabar Hills mansion) in India was lost to the family
after the partition of India and Pakistan.

SHE BREAKS HER FAST WITH A PINCH OF SALT

and walks into the sea
with her Koran, and again,
the jute-fan vendors, the *sherbet-wallahs*
are saying: She must
be out of her mind to recite the book
knee-deep in water.
The tourists (on whose mirrored
sunglasses she multiplies)
are alarmed:
Is she dispatching
killer waves?

She sees
in the moon's cavity
where its fetus was,
her lost son –
his Navy uniform
darkened by amniotic water.

It's in Sleep
A Soul Will Know Itself

I am neither a Persian
nor a Mughal miniature;
no toothless gazelle, ivory hand fan,
sitar tremolo, rose syrup,
no tiger hunt, velvet howdah,
sweltering divan of poems.

I looked but did not find myself
under the desert's back lit
piercing clocks, its lexicon of loss,
lures and winds
of woven fragrance.

I was never
a black and white begum
blooming out of a soufflé
of silk *gharara*,
leaning on a gold cane,
nor a sepia Sahab Bahadur
with his shoe on the lap
of a native.

I never rode a motorbike through a tunnel
under a river.
No cigarette in my mouth
nor a niqab pressed to my nose.
When I close my eyes
I am the ripped tire
rolling beside a barefoot boy
with a stick
I spin to his whim
across a rocky,
jasmine scented hill.

Nice! / Q?

NIGHT OF THE EID MOON

*E*ver-elusive moons
And that mistakable scent of paper:
Apple rinds? Pencil peel? Rain-soak?

In the henna bowl
the scent
of a full lunar month:
the time it took my mother to sew
my *Hyderabadi*
with its primrose silk over-shirt
shiny trimmed sleeves
stitched to a muslin slip
The two-toned veil
last to be ironed and draped over my desk
the night before
Its sequins
edging the slippery rim of wakefulness

falling like shrunken stars through a basin
of smoke
where the chatter of child-sized glass
bangles will amplify
Don't Hate Me: I'm Muslim
It will be another time
Another place

(Ramadan, 2010: Among the protestors of Koran-burning was a little boy who
held up a sign saying *Don't Hate me: I'm Muslim*)

60

A Mirror in the City Square

BURNT POEM

To the wizard-black wick
of the candle's twisted vanilla

The thick air rolled into a snore
Walls caked with layers of sleep
Wet towels slumped on the oak slats of the bench

My mouth
is hooked by the past tense

Wordless with the moon's meat on my tongue
I am no more than shadow
Forget I said anything

WAR

Tremolo of teacups
Scissoring sirens

Two streets ripped apart

Flesh-eating clocks
Clock-eating wheels

A time of boots
A town of tires

The night has accrued sap
to trap us — *me?* —
in its amber

GHAZAL

Human, the word, came from the word for love in Arabic, *breath*
from love in Hebrew. Language: purple mass, body without breath.

Our bread came from the same oven and we drank from the same deep well
rimmed with the name of God, over whom we fought with every breath.

You saved our salt to sprinkle on this, my gaping wound. I saw your bullet
cross the steel-blue night. I woke up sweating and short of breath.

A small button killed thousands and we never saw the blood-filled Euphrates.
Instead, the news-caster's pearls, her mouth, vowels crisply shaped by breath.

Fresh milk, a shawl for warmth, a drop of medicine, paper to relieve
the heart's burden, a place to pray; things we wished for, other than breath.

There is a sigh squeezed between bricks of our house. Our names lie flat
and dead. Take the key to unlock air, to waken the sleeping breath.

The stars have become our sins, bullet holes edged with yellow poison. Look
at us going down the drain, into the stench of discord. Hold your breath.

IMAN

Come be spun in the nightly vortex
where I am Sarai's child some times
And sometimes Hagar's
My mothers–
their golden dust
rises between us
when Jerusalem's trees morph into green tanks

Your loquacious mouth
shapes missiles with my name on them
And of both my mothers
Come kiss each missile on the forehead
before you strike this house
Poems that were doors
will forever close and split
into ancient pebbles
Come like rain falling on the tanks

Your sleeves dry and mighty
with no tears to wipe
Come turn in my grave
where every flower ticks like a bomb

(Iman was a Palestinian girl who was sprayed with bullets by Israeli soldiers as she walked to school, Rafah, 2004; Her name means "faith")

PETRUSHKA

> Even beyond the mountains there are human beings.
> —*Russian Folk Proverb*

*L*ights
smashed on snow.
Electricity swirling like a carnival song
in one's head—
painted on such a large scale
each dancing nerve offers a rhyme,
then shrivels with a blue spark.
St. Petersburg has the face of a clock
wound by the wise,
misread by the crowd.

Was it sawdust
for a body that was Petrushka's mischance,
or having a soul?

A puppet could hang from a pendulum
in the city square, and its sway would make
no heads turn either way.

It is the soul that burns.

When light breaks
on this snow again, there will be some bodies lolling,
more souls burning. The crowd will be its own mirror.
An untampered clock will remind
that beyond the Hindukush
there are human beings.

U.S. Air Strikes

In the four minutes
it took me to mince the cloves,
dump the tea leaves
in the rose bush,
and soap the carafe,
a whole city was lost.

There were feet still in school shoes,
limp flesh singing into satchels,
clinging to a post, a shattered clock.
The children, if not orphaned
were purpled beyond recognition.

Orders had been carried down,
one signal igniting another.
And a man had let a deafening rhapsody
guide his young hand to drop
a five hundred pound bomb
on a mosque.

Just when I finished rinsing the carafe,
a whole city was under cement dust and smoke,
and I thought I heard screaming behind walls of fire
in the kettle's sharp whistle,
just when I added the cloves,
the last green lime.

GUANTANAMO

χ

A guard forces you to urinate on yourself
Another barks out louder than his dog
the names of your sisters
who live in the delicate nest
of a ruby-throated hummingbird
Each will be a skeleton he says

Was there someone who gave you
seven almonds for memory,
a teaspoon of honey every morning?
Cardamom tea before bed?
Someone who starched your shirts
in rice water, then ironed them?
Held your chin
To say the send-off prayer
before school?

You're tied to a metal coil
And memory
is a burnt wire.

Paris Ghazal

Named for a blind man, city of shadow and angle, silhouetted by sun-lit lace,
luxuriate in your finesse, in cakes, silk tissue curtains and doll-delicate lace!

There has been a time for the gallows, for heads snapped
at the guillotine. And a time for chiffon, soufflé, Chantilly lace.

I saw slender-boned Nefertari cleaning the urinal in a café's toilet,
On her finger, a Lapis ring, on her smooth neck, heavy gold lace.

Rain brings the thought of poets with empty pockets who sang this city
to glory. Pavements are wet, traffic lights reflecting like colored lace.

The Seine flows alongside book-stalls, avenues scented with warm sugar.
Here, I'll catch the one word that forever allows me to weave it like lace.

They still clamor for bread, at the feet of gilded statues of heroes.
History has one eye open, the other is only a socket covered with lace.

MOSQUÉE DE PARIS

Ablution water,
opal
on a worshipper's
slipper left by the doorstep:
She will travel far
and return before its sparkle has dropped.

Gold and ink on parchment
dyed blue
speaks of duty to the widow and the wayfarer.

Light caught on pink marble
swirls into an open ear.

Eggs in the outstretched hands
of an old woman in Kabul
For the widows of New York
The American author takes them trembling
Insha'Allah.

If there were no kindness
conversation would be useless,
Rumi says. His guides:
A goldsmith, a desert wanderer, a scribe.

Stitched to silence,
you and I wander the same places,
wearing zipped shoes. ___ ⁊

Santa Ana Fires

A toaster fire snatches a curtain
Then snares the house in a gasp

My dream is combustible
Smoke everywhere
And everything catching

All night the television rages   latching on half-sleep
I unhook my eyes and toss them into the flames

A newscaster   the height of a chokecherry tree
wears her pendant over a fire-proof vest

reads the names of the war-dead instead
of California properties burned down
Iraqi names folded like hands
Forked like roads

Every name   a beating heart

For days she stands in the noxious air
losing her polish   her posture

reading a list long as an umbilical cord
joining us to the sun

In the Piazza

A tentative note on the accordion
Across the mural a weak dawn
Fractured columns of light
on the goddess of war with a ridiculously small head
and metallic horses sculpted in unnatural proportions

There are people in the piazza too
The accordion player's wife
a banker finishing his coffee
a young nun in a bubble jacket looking for keys
in her backpack and my baby chewing on his terry lion

There are boys running after pigeons
that carry rainbows around their necks — *shifts to metaphor intensifies*
The sun humiliates statues of gunmen   *the emotion/mystery*
that dwarf us with their big ideas
Us and our small music

SCRABBLE

For Marjorie Rosenfeld

Hide across
Hibiscus down
The scrabble tiles are
like cubes of restaurant butter

Pocket bread waits
for them both on a burnt–orange
ceramic plate

Home across
Hate down

One makes *Scud*
the other *Keys*

Our children will make war   — *nice break*
a thing of the past
Imagine across
shine down   ✗

74

Anadolu

At the end of the river, a woman makes bread.
A shady tree will be easy to find here
and anything you've lost,
if it matters, will bob up
right by the small boats.
Neither the flowers
nor the fruits are without a thin fringe
of brown. Clay pots shimmer. Every thing
is aging, with a sweet center.
My cold desk, wafting in the Bosporus,
is circled by honey bees.

AUTHOR BIOGRAPHY

Shadab Zeest Hashmi is a Pushcart nominee and winner of the San Diego Book Award for poetry for *Baker of Tarifa*—a book based on the history of interfaith tolerance in Al Andalus (Muslim Spain). Her work has been included in the *Seeds of Peace* concert with the award-winning Al Andalus Ensemble, in the film *Cruzando Lineas: Crossing Lines*, and has been translated into Urdu by Pakistan Academy of Arts and Letters. She has presented her series of poems and photographs titled "Across the Windowsill" at San Diego Museum of Art. She has served as an editor for the annual *Magee Park Anthology* and the online journal *MahMag World Literature* and has taught as a visiting professor in the MFA program at San Diego State University. She has published her poetry and prose in numerous journals worldwide and represents Pakistan on *UniVerse: A United Nations of Poetry*.

Cover and Illustrations by Michele Guieu
www.micheleguieu.com

San Francisco Bay area based / French born artist Michele Guieu uses both traditional and nontraditional media in her work: murals and painting, drawing, photography and video. Her work has been shown in exhibitions at venues such as Mac Paris (France), Currents 2012: the Santa Fe International New Media Festival, the San Diego Museum of Art, The California Center for the Arts, the Oceanside Museum of Art, Rosalux Gallery, Le Musee des Merveilles (France), Art Produce Gallery, The San Diego Art Institute, Kaleid Gallery, ZERO1 Biennial and Subzero Festival.

CPSIA information can be obtained at www.ICGtesting.com
Printed in the USA
BVOW040450250213

314024BV00001B/3/P